Emilie S Coles

Mission band Hymnal

Emilie S Coles

Mission band Hymnal

ISBN/EAN: 9783743340459

Manufactured in Europe, USA, Canada, Australia, Japa

Cover: Foto ©ninafisch / pixelio.de

Manufactured and distributed by brebook publishing software
(www.brebook.com)

Emilie S Coles

Mission band Hymnal

THE

MISSION BAND

HYMNAL.

MDCCCLXXIX.

DEAR YOUNG FRIENDS, MEMBERS OF MISSION BANDS, HELPERS IN THE GOOD WORK OF PUBLISHING THE GOSPEL TO EVERY CREATURE:

This little Hymnal, designed for your use, is to you affectionately inscribed. It is gratifying to know that the number of your Bands, already large, and confined to no one denomination, is constantly increasing. The high testimony that you have already received is full of encouragement. In view of the fact, that at all your meetings, singing forms, very appropriately, an important part of the exercises, the need of a special collection of Hymns has been greatly felt by some of your number. To meet this want, this Manual of Sacred Songs has been prepared. It consists largely of Hymns never before brought together. A considerable number, having been written expressly for this work and adapted to favorite tunes, are now published for the first time. Inasmuch as you represent all ages, some being older, others younger, the aim has been to furnish Hymns suitable for all. Some of the Hymns are directly missionary in their character, while others are only indirectly so; by which is meant, that while they contain no direct reference to missions, the end in view, it is believed, is not less effectually secured, by their fitness to excite gratitude and love to Christ, and zeal for His cause.

In conclusion, let me improve this hallowed time, devoted to the singing of sweet Christmas carols by the glad voices of children, and the general interchange of happy greetings and good wishes, to send you my own loving salutation in that form, which the blessed Saviour Himself used and taught His disciples to use— "Peace be with you!" that "peace which passeth all understanding." F. S. C.

SCOTCH PLAINS, N. J.,
Christmas, 1878.

1   MISSIONARY CHANT. L. M.

LIFT up your heads, ye gates! swing wide,
  Ye dazzling portals of the morn!
Forth let the Filial Godhead ride
  On wings of cherubim upborne!

2 Nor dare, thou flushed and flattered East!
  The Sun of Righteousness to stay,
Now that the long dark night hath ceased.
  And souls are hungry for the day.

3 On mountain tops, bright heralds stand,
  With beautiful and shining feet.
And publish over sea and land
  The welcome tidings glad and sweet :

4 He comes! The sky is all on fire :
  We see the bannered pomp unfurled,
The advancing Splendor rushing higher
  To flood and overflow the world !

ABRAHAM COLES.

Is. 9. 6.

2   STELLA.   L. M.

" WHAT means this glory round our feet,"
      The Magi mused, "more bright than morn ? "
And voices chanted strong and sweet,
   "To-day, the Prince of Peace is born ! "

2 "What means this star," the shepherds said,
   " That brightens through the rocky glen ? "
And angels answering overhead,
   Sang "Peace on earth, good will to men ! "

3 'Tis eighteen hundred years and more,
   Since those sweet oracles were dumb ;
We wait for Him like them of yore ;
   Alas ! He seems so long to come !

4 But it was said in words of gold,
   No time or sorrow e'er shall dim,
That little children might be bold,
   In perfect trust to come to Him.

5 All round about our feet shall shine
   A light, like that the wise men saw,
If we our loving wills incline
   To that sweet Life which is the Law.

6

6 So shall we learn to understand
   The simple faith of shepherds, then,
And kindly clasping hand in hand,
   Sing, " Peace on earth, good will to men ! "

JAMES RUSSELL LOWELL.

3   ORIOLA. C. M. Double.

IT came upon the midnight clear,
   That glorious song of old,
From angels bending near the earth
   To touch their harps of gold :
" Peace to the earth, good will to man,
   From heaven's all gracious King : "
The earth in solemn stillness lay,
   To hear the angels sing.

2 Still thro' the cloven skies they come,
   With peaceful wings unfurled ;
And still celestial music floats
   O'er all the weary world ;
Above its sad and lowly plains
   They bend on heavenly wing,
And ever o'er its Babel sounds
   The blessed angels sing !

3 O ye, beneath life's crushing load,
    Whose forms are bending low,
Who toil along the climbing way,
    With painful steps and slow,
Look up! for glad and golden hours
    Come swiftly on the wing :
O rest beside the weary road,
    And hear the angels sing !

4 For, lo, the days are hastening on,
    By prophet-bards foretold,
When with the ever-circling years
    Comes round the age of gold !
When peace shall over all the earth
    Its final splendors fling,
And the whole world send back the song
    Which now the angels sing.

EDMUND H. SEARS.

4

AGATE. 11.

NIGHT'S canopy over Judea now hung :
   The harp of the minstrel lay still and unstrung ;
The shepherds together sat watching the fold,
While round them reigned darkness and silence and cold.

2 And now, in their midst, shines an angel of light ;
Quick vanishes Fear at the radiant sight !
And hark, in the words of their own native tongue,
" Good tidings of joy," by the angels are sung.

3 " This day, in the city of David is born
A Saviour, whose birth is Redemption's glad morn :
No longer through darkness and doubt shall ye grope,
In Bethlehem's manger lies Israel's Hope ! "

4 A chorus angelic re-echoes in Heaven
The glorious news to the meek shepherds given :
" Peace, peace and good will unto earth ! " is their song,
While praises to God the loud pæan prolong.

ELIZABETH C. KINNEY.

5   RIFTED ROCK.   8, 7.

HE that lay in lowly manger,
    Now is known as Heaven's King ;
What but angels sang, aforetime,
Now have men been taught to sing :

2 " God have glory, in the highest :
Peace on earth, good will towards men:
Over all the tide of ages,
Ever now as it was then."

Acts 10. 36.

3 Lo, He came, the Lord of glory !
Born and cradled in a stall :
Sure He had but scanty welcome,
Seeing He was Lord of all.

4 Yet, in sooth, He sought no other ;
Nor to earth for homage came ;
Here he took the form of servant,
Here he bared the cheek to shame.

5 Not of this world was His Kingdom,
He lived not at monarch's cost ;
He sought not the known and honored,
But He came to seek the lost.

6 Glory, worship, love and service,
To the Blessed One in Three ;
As it was in the beginning,
Is, and evermore shall be.

ROBERT LOWELL.

6

ROSEFIELD.   7, 6.

A S with gladness men of old
Did the guiding star behold ;
As with joy they hailed its light
Leading onward, beaming bright ;
So, most gracious Lord, may we
Evermore be led to Thee.

2 Holy Jesus, every day
Keep us in the narrow way;
And, when earthly things are past,
Bring our ransomed souls at last
Where they need no star to guide,
Where no clouds Thy glory hide.

3 In the heavenly country bright.
Need they no created light;
Thou, its Life, its Joy, its Crown,
Thou, its Sun which goes not down;
There, forever, may we sing
Hallelujahs to our King.

WILLIAM C. DIX.

DOXOLOGY.

Praise the name of God most high:
Praise Him all below the sky;
Praise Him all ye heavenly host,
Father, Son, and Holy Ghost:
As through countless ages past,
Evermore His praise shall last!

Rev. 22. 16.

7   Evan.   C. M.

A S shadows cast by cloud and sun,
    Flit o'er the summer grass,
So, in Thy sight, Almighty One!
    Earth's generations pass.

2 And while the years, an endless host,
    Come passing swiftly on,
The brightest names that earth can boast,
    Just glisten and are gone.

3 Yet doth the star of Bethlehem shed
    A lustre pure and sweet ;
And still it leads, as once it led,
    To the Messiah's feet.

4 And deeply, at this latter day,
    Our hearts rejoice to see
How children, guided by its ray,
    Come to the Saviour's knee.

5 O Father, may that holy Star
    Grow every year more bright,
And send its glorious beams afar,
    To fill the world with light.

WILLIAM CULLEN BRYANT.

Zech. 14 9.

[As a leaf typifies the whole tree from which it has fallen, so does a lofty snow-capped mountain at the equator represent the whole earth in miniature. Indeed, the globe may be compared to two great mountains set base to base at the equator, the summit of the one being the north pole and the other the south pole. In ascending Orizaba, or any other of the giant peaks of the Andes of Quito, the traveler passes successively through all the climates of the earth, the seasons of the year, and the zones of vegetable and animal life. He can see, when he has reached the summit, what is elsewhere spread horizontally over the earth's surface, and over the whole year, vertically represented along the side of the mountain below him; while above him, if he be there over night, he can behold the whole firmament of stars, those of the northern as well as those of the southern hemisphere—the Southern Cross and the Magellanic clouds around the Antarctic pole, and the constellation of the Plough around the Arctic pole. Such a mountain summit is the watch-tower of creation, from which with overpowering emotion the eye may embrace, in one glorious view, the whole universe of things.]

8   INGLESIDE.   C. M.

THERE is one spot where man may stand,
     And at a single glance,
All glories of the sky and land
     Behold in rapture's trance.

2 The heavens unroll their mystic scroll
     Of stars above his head;
The Cross and Plough at either pole
     Their rays together shed.

3 All seasons meet beneath the same
     Triumphal arch of blue;
And all earth's charms combine to frame
     One picture to his view.

4 Oh could we find some central peak,
   High in the world of soul,
From whence the broken views we seek
   Might blend in one great whole ;

5 Where we, above all doubt, might stand
   In air as crystal clear,
And every mystery understand,
   And bring all distance near.

6 We stand upon a point so low,
   We see of earth and sky
But one small arc ; in part we know ;
   In part we prophesy.

7 In vain we long for larger views,
   Which loftier heights impart ;
The limits of our life refuse
   The wishes of our heart.

8 While here, the wisest sage must live
   By faith and not by sight ;
For duty only, Heaven will give
   Enough of guiding light.

John 1. 9.

9 But when, at last, from life's dark road,
We climb heaven's heights serene,
All light upon the hill of God,
In God's light shall be seen.

10 All kingdoms of the truth shall there,
To tearless eyes be shown;
And dwelling in that purer air,
We'll know as we are known.

HUGH MACMILLAN.

9 HOLMAN. 8, 6, 8.

O NORTH, with all thy vales of green!
O South, with all thy palms!
From peopled towns and fields between
Uplift the voice of psalms.
Raise, ancient East! the anthem high,
And let the youthful West reply.

2 Lo! in the clouds of heaven appears
God's well beloved Son.
He brings a train of brighter years,
His kingdom is begun.
He comes a guilty world to bless
With mercy, truth, and righteousness.

3 O Father! haste the promised hour,
  When at His feet shall lie
All rule, authority, and power,
  Beneath the ample sky;
When he shall reign from pole to pole,
The Lord of every human soul.

4 When all shall heed the words He said,
  Amid their daily cares,
And by the loving life He led,
  Shall strive to pattern theirs;
And He who conquered Death shall win
The mightier conquest over Sin.

WILLIAM CULLEN BRYANT

10   BARBY. C. M.

JESUS is God! the glorious bands
  Of holy angels sing
Songs of adoring praise to Him,
  Their Maker and their King.

2 He was true God in Bethlehem's crib;
  On Calvary's cross, true God:
He, who in heaven eternal reigned,
  In time on earth abode.

Rom. 9. 5.

3 Jesus is God! oh, could I now
　　But compass land and sea,
To teach and tell this single truth,
　　How happy should I be!

4 Oh, had I but an angel's voice,
　　I would proclaim so loud:
Jesus, the good, the beautiful
　　Is Everlasting God.

FREDERICK W. FABER.

HARWELL. 8, 7.

AT Thy feet. our God and Father,
　　Who hast blessed us all our days.
We with grateful hearts would gather.
　　And begin the year with praise:
Praise for light so brightly shining
　　On our steps from heaven above:
Praise for mercies daily twining
　　Round us golden cords of love.

2 Jesus. for Thy love most tender
　　On the cross for sinners shown.
We would praise Thee, and surrender
　　All our hearts to be Thine own.

With so blest a Friend provided,
  We upon our way would go,
Sure of being safely guided,
  Guarded well from every foe.

3 Every day will be the brighter,
  When Thy gracious face we see ;
Every burden will be lighter,
  When we know it comes from Thee.
Spread Thy love's broad banner o'er us,
  Give us strength to serve and wait,
Till Thy glory breaks before us,
  Through the City's open gate.

J. D. BURNS.

12   MALVERN. L. M.

I ALWAYS love to praise Thee, Lord ;
  I cannot sing to show my art ;
I could not sing the solemn word
  Except I felt it with my heart.

2 I try to keep my spirit clean,
  But oh, I feel it is not so,
And oft my sight of things unseen,
  Is darkened by my sin I know.

18

Cant. 5. 16.

3 But when I go to heaven above,
  I then shall see Him face to face,
And for the fullness of that love
  Impurity can find no place.

4 I cannot always here below
  Sing out Thy praises as I would ;
The music will not always flow
  As unto Thee it ever should.

5 But there the singing will be grand,
  And I, I hope, shall know that song
The pure alone can understand ;
  Let me not wait, Lord, very long.

A. J. MASON.

13   EVEN ME. 8, 7, 3.

O UT the mouths of babes and sucklings,
  Thou canst perfect praise to Thee !
Wilt thou not accept the worship,
  Humbly rendered, Lord, by me ?
      Even me.

2 Things that to the wise are hidden,
  Children's eyes are made to see ;
Thee to know is life eternal,
  O reveal Thyself to me !
      Even me.

19

Is. 40. 10.

3 Thou hast given me power of loving,
   Give me power of serving Thee,
Is there not some humble service
   Which can now be done by me?
               Even me.

4 Hands and feet should ne'er grow weary
   When employed, dear Lord, for Thee;
Tongue should never cease the telling
   Of Thy grace who diedst for me,
               Even me.

5 Infant mouths need not be silent,
   Stammering lips can publish Thee,
Sound Thy name o'er land and ocean,
   Be it sounded, Lord, by me!
               Even me.

ABRAHAM COLES.

14   WILMOT.   8, 7.

LITTLE hearts, O Lord, may love Thee,
   Little minds may learn Thy ways;
Little hands and feet may serve Thee,
   Little voices sing Thy praise.

2 Little ones we stand before Thee,
   Larger shall we yearly grow;
Help us ever to adore Thee,
   All through life Thy grace to show.

T. H. STOCKTON.

15   THATCHER.   G. M.

I OFTEN say my prayers;
     But do I ever pray?
And do the wishes of my heart
     Go with the words I say?

2 I may as well kneel down
     And worship gods of stone,
As offer to the living God
     A prayer of words alone.

3 For words without the heart
     The Lord will never hear;
Nor will He to those lips attend
     Whose prayers are not sincere.

                     JOHN BURTON.

16   JERUSALEM. C. M.

A MID the blue and starry sky,
     A group of Hours one even
Met, as they took their upward flight
     Into the highest heaven:

2 Commissioned each to bear above,
     Whatever had been done
By little children good or bad,
     Since the last rising sun.

B

3 And some had gold and purple wings,
    Some drooped like faded flowers
And sadly soared to tell the tale
    That they were misspent hours.

4 Some glowed with rosy hopes and smiles,
    And some had many a tear ;
Others had some kind words and acts
    To carry upward there.

5 A shining hour with golden plumes
    Was laden with a deed
Of generous sacrifice a child,
    Had done for one in need.

6 And one was bearing up a prayer,
    A little child had said,
All full of penitence and love,
    While kneeling by his bed.

7 And thus they glided on and gave
    Their records dark and bright
To Him who marks each passing hour
    Of childhood's day and night.

Ja 2. 1.

8 O let us all remember how
　Each hour is on its way,
Bearing its own report to heaven
　Of all we do and say.

MRS. GORDON.

SICILIAN HYMN. 8, 7.

L ORD, a little band and lowly,
　 We are come to sing to Thee;
Thou art great and high and holy,
　O how solemn we should be!

2 Fill our hearts with thoughts of Jesus,
　And of heaven where He is gone,
And let nothing ever please us,
　He would grieve to look upon.

3 For we know, the Lord of glory
　Always sees what children do,
And is writing now the story
　Of our thoughts and actions, too.

4 Let our sins be all forgiven,
　Make us fear whate'er is wrong;
Lead us on our way to heaven,
　There to sing a nobler song.

John 12. 15.

18   RATHBUN.   8, 7.

WE are children, happy children,
    Singing, singing, as we go,
'Tis our Father's hand that leads us,
    Leads us through this world below.

2 When a sinful world around us
    Tempts our little feet to stray,
By His Spirit He will keep us
    In the straight and narrow way.

3 If we try to follow Jesus,
    Try to serve Him here below,
Where He lives and reigns forever,
    Singing, singing, we shall go.

19   ST. JOHN'S.   C. M.

HOSANNAS were by children sung,
    When Jesus was on earth ;
Then surely we are not too young
    To sound His praises forth.

2 The Lord is great, the Lord is good,
    He feeds us from His store
With earthly and with heavenly food,
    And saves us evermore.

3 We thank Him for His precious Word.
We thank Him for His grace,
Well may the praises of our Lord
Be sung in every place.

GRATITUDE. L. M.

THIS Book unfolds Jehovah's mind,
This Voice salutes in accents kind,
This Friend will all your need supply,
This Fountain sends forth streams of joy ,

2 This Mine affords us boundless wealth,
This Good Physician gives us health,
This Sun renews and warms the soul,
This Sword both wounds and makes us whole.

3 This Letter shows our sins forgiven,
This Guide conducts us safe to heaven,
This Charter has been sealed with blood,
This Volume is the Word of God.

MARTH. 7, 3.

JESUS, when he left the sky,
And for sinners came to die.
In His mercy passed not by,
Little ones like me.

2 Mothers, then, the Saviour sought
In the places where He taught,
And to Him their children brought,
Little ones like me.

3 Did the Saviour say them nay ?
No, He kindly bade them stay ;
Suffered none to turn away
Little ones like me.

4 'Twas for them His life He gave,
To redeem them from the grave :
Jesus able is to save
Little ones like me.

22   Over There. 8, 7, 3.

DO the children know of Jesus,
    Over there, over there ?
Have they heard redemption's story,
    Over there, over there ?

Chorus—Ah ! they know not of the Saviour,
     Of His wondrous love and care ;
Still they sit in heathen darkness,
    Without Jesus over there.

2 Do the children pray to Jesus,
  Over there ; over there ?
Do they seek his kind protection
  Over there, over there ?—Cho.

3 Do the children sing of Jesus,
  Over there, over there ?
Do they chant his praises ever
  Over there, over there ?—Cho.

4 Do the children work for Jesus,
  Over there, over there ?
Do they labor for His glory,
  Over there, over there ?—Cho.

5 Do the children live for Jesus,
  Over there, over there ?
Do they love the precious Saviour,
  Over there, over there ?—Cho.

H. T. B.

23   Heber.   C. M.

I THANK the goodness and the grace
  That on my birth have smiled,
And made me in these latter days
  A happy, Christian child.

1 John 5. 20.

2 I was not born. as thousands are,
  Where God is never known,
And taught to say a useless prayer
  To gods of wood and stone.

3 My God, I thank Thee, who hast planned
  A better lot for me,
And placed me in this favored land,
  Where I may hear of Thee.

ISAAC WATTS.

24   ZEPHYR.   L. M.

O HOLY Father, just and true
  Are all Thy works and words and ways,
And unto Thee alone are due
  Thanksgiving and eternal praise.

2 As children of Thy gracious care,
  We veil the eye, we bend the knee;
With broken words of praise and prayer,
  Father and God, we come to Thee.

3 For those to whom Thy loving word
  Of light and love is never given;
For those whose ears have never heard
  The promise and the hope of heaven;

4 For broken heart, and clouded mind.
　Whereon no human mercies fall ;
Oh, be Thy gracious love inclined,
　Who, as a father, pitiest all !

5 And grant, O Father! that the time
　Of Earth's deliverance may be near.
When every land, and tongue, and clime,
　The message of Thy love shall hear.

JOHN G. WHITTIER.

25
PLEYEL'S HYMN.
L ITTLE givers come and bring,
　Tribute to your Heavenly King,
Many offerings though but small,
Make a large one from you all.

2 Little givers! do your part,
With a glad and willing heart,
Give to all the darkened earth
Tidings of a heavenly birth.

26
LYONS. 7.
W E bring the bright pennies,
　They're little we know ;
But love going with them,
　To dollars they'll grow ;

2 As much as this surely,
  We children can see,
If there were no pennies,
  No dollars there'd be.

27 Boardman. C. M.

WHAT if the little rain should say,
    "So small a drop as I
Can ne'er refresh those thirsty fields
  I'll tarry in the sky!"

2 What if a shining beam at noon
  Should in its fountain stay,
Because its feeble light alone
  Cannot create a day.

3 Doth not each rain drop help to form
  The cool refreshing shower?
And every ray of light to warm
  And beautify the flower?

4 Go thou and strive to do thy share;
  One talent—less than thine,
Improved with steady zeal and care
  Would gain rewards divine.

Cutter.

28   LITTLE THINGS.   6. 5.

L ITTLE dropsof water,
   Little grains of sand,
Make the mighty ocean
   And the beauteous land.

2. And the little moments,
   Humble though they be,
Make the mighty ages
   Of eternity.

3 Little deeds of kindness,
   Little words of love,
Make our earth an Eden
   Like the heaven above.

4 Little seeds of mercy,
   Sown by youthful hands,
Grow to bless the nations
   Far in heathen lands.

EBEN C. BREWER.

29   ADORATION.   6, 5.

S EE the rivers flowing
   Downward to the sea,
Pouring all their treasures
   Bountiful and free ;

THE REWARDER

Mat. 16. 27.

Yet to help their giving
  Hidden springs arise ;
Or, if need be, showers
  Feed them from the skies.

2 Watch the princely flowers
  Their rich fragrance spread,
Load the air with perfumes
  From their beauty shed ;
Yet their lavish spending
  Leaves them not in dearth,
With fresh life replenished
  By their mother earth.

3 Give thy heart's best treasures ;
  From fair nature learn ;
Give thy love and ask not,
  Wait not a return,
And the more thou spendest
  From thy little store,
With a double bounty
  God will give thee more.

ADELAIDE A. PROCTOR.

30   HEROLD.   7.

THUS said Jesus : "Go and do
  As thou would'st be done unto ! "

3 2

Here thy perfect duty see
All that God requires of thee.

2 Wouldst thou, when thy faults are known,
Wish that pardon should be shown.
Be forgiving then and do
As thou wouldst be done unto.

3 Shouldst thou helpless be and poor,
Wouldst thou not for aid implore?
Think of others then and be
What thou wouldst they should to thee.

4 For compassion if thou call,
Be compassionate to all ;
If thou wouldst affection find,
Be affectionate and kind.

5 If thou wouldst obtain the love
Of thy gracious God above,
Then to all His children be
What thou wouldst they should to thee.

W ROSCOE.

31   HENDON. 7.

LAMB of God I look to Thee,
Thou shalt my example be;
Thou art gentle, meek and mild,
Thou wast once a little child.

2 Fain I would be as Thou art,
Give me Thy obedient heart;
Thou art pitiful and kind,
Let me have Thy loving mind.

3 Let me above all fulfil,
As Thou dost, Thy Father's will;
Never Thy good Spirit grieve,
Only to Thy glory live.

4 Loving Jesus, gentle Lamb,
In Thy gracious hands I am,
Make me Saviour what Thou art,
Live Thyself within my heart.

CHARLES WESLEY.

32 WOODWORTH. L. M.

THE lambs of Jesus! who are they
But children that believe and pray?
That keep God's laws and ask His grace
And seek a heavenly dwelling place!

2 The lambs of Jesus! they are meek,
The words of peace and truth they speak;
To all God's creatures they are kind,
And, like their Lord, of gentle mind.

3 The lambs of Jesus ! oh, that we
Might of that blessed number be ;
Lord, take us early to Thy love,
And lead us to the fold above.

33   BEULAH. 7.

L ITTLE travelers Zionward,
    Each one entering into rest,
In the kingdom of your Lord,
    In the mansion of the blest :
There to welcome Jesus waits ;
    Gives the crowns His followers win ;
Lift your heads, ye golden gates,
    Let the little travelers in !

2 Who are they whose little feet,
    Pacing life's dark journey through,
Now have reach'd the heavenly seat,
    They have ever kept in view ?
" I, from Greenland's frozen land : "
    " I, from India's sultry plain : "
" I, from Afric's barren sand ; "
    " I, from islands of the main."

3 " All our earthly journey past,
    Every tear and pain gone by,
We're together met at last,
    At the portal of the sky."
Each the welcome " Come" awaits
    Conquerors over death and sin ;
Lift your heads, ye golden gates !
    Let the little travelers in !

JAMES EDMESTON.

34   OLMUTZ. S. M.

D IVINE, Eternal Word !
    Who makest sucklings wise :
The Alphabet of heavenly lore !
    The Primer of the skies !

2 Our letters thus to be,
    Thou didst from heaven descend :
Alpha, Omega, First and Last,
    Beginning and the End !

3 Like children we would sit,
    Jesus, at Thy dear feet,
And learn of Thee the rudiments,
    So simple and so sweet.

4 Thou, Christ, art very God!
  Once taught Thy name to spell.
Delighted we decipher it
  On all Thy works as well.

5 In Thee, in Thee, we find
  The key that all unlocks ;
The secrets of the starry heavens,
  The writing on the rocks.

ABRAHAM COLES

35   FULTON. 7.

SAVIOUR! teach me, day by day,
  Love's sweet lesson to obey ;
Sweeter lesson cannot be,
Loving Him who first loved me.

2 With a childlike heart of love,
At Thy bidding may I move :
Prompt to serve and follow Thee,
Loving Him who first loved me.

3 Teach me all Thy steps to trace,
Strong to follow in Thy grace :
Learning how to love from Thee,
Loving Him who first loved me.

C

4 Love in loving finds employ ;
In obedience all her joy ;
Ever new that joy will be,
Loving Him who first loved me.

5 Thus may I rejoice to show
That I feel the love I owe :
Singing, till Thy face I see,
Of His love who first loved me.

36   Clifford. C. M.

THE memory of Jesus' name
  Is past expression sweet ;
At each dear mention, hearts aflame
  With quicker pulses beat.

2 But sweet, above all sweetest things
  Creation can afford,
That sweetness which His presence brings,
  The vision of the Lord.

3 Sweeter than His dear Name is nought ;
  None, worthier of laud,
Was ever sung, or heard, or thought,
  Than Jesus, Son of God.

4 Thou hope to those of contrite heart!
To those who ask. how kind!
To those who seek how good Thou art!
But what to those who find?

5 No heart is able to conceive,
Nor tongue nor pen express ;
Who tries it only can believe
How choice that blessedness!

BERNARD OF CLAIRVAUX, Translated by ABRAHAM COLES.

37   CLEANSING FOUNTAIN.   C. M.

O H. for a thousand tongues to sing
    My great Redeemer's praise,
The glories of my God and King,
    The triumphs of His grace.

2 My gracious Master and my God,
    Assist me to proclaim,
To spread through all the earth abroad
    The honors of Thy name.

CHARLES WESLEY.

38   CREATION.   L. M.

I SING the Shepherd of the sheep.
    Who, for the love He bare the fold.
Did wade through sorrows dark and deep,
    And freely give His life of old.

39

2 I sing the love, so strange, so sweet,
    That sought the lost, until it found,
With aching heart and bleeding feet,
    And flowing tears that wet the ground.

3 I sing the goodness of our God,
    The patient pity and the grace
That left no dreadful path untrod
    To seek and save the human race.

4 Great Shepherd of the nations! Thou
    Bishop of souls, go forth to find
Thy scattered flock! O, gather now
    The straying millions of mankind!

ABRAHAM COLES.

39   GOLDEN HILL. S. M.

O GOD of sovereign grace,
    We bow before Thy throne,
And plead for all the human race,
    The merits of Thy Son.

Spread through the earth, O Lord,
    The knowledge of Thy ways,
And let all lands with joy record
    The great Redeemer's praise.

Lu. 2. 32.

40   LABAN.   S. M.

THY name, almighty Lord,
     Shall sound through distant lands ;
Great is Thy grace, and sure Thy word ;
     Thy truth forever stands.

2 Far be Thine honor spread,
     And long Thy praise endure,
Till morning light and evening shade
     Shall be exchanged no more.

                        ISAAC WATTS.

41   WANDERER.   L. M. DOUBLE.

THE Banyan of the Indian isle
     Spreads deeply down its massive root,
And spreads its branching life abroad,
     And bends to earth its scarlet fruit ;
But when the branches reach the ground,
     They firmly plant themselves again,
They rise and spread and droop and root,
     An ever green and endless chain.

2 And so the Church of Jesus Christ,
     The blessed Banyan of our God,
Fast rooted upon Zion 's mount,
     Has sent its sheltering arms abroad ;

And every branch that from it springs,
  In sacred beauty spreading wide
As low it bends to bless the earth,
  Still plants another by its side.

3 Long as the world itself shall last
  The sacred Banyan still shall spread,
From clime to clime, from age to age,
  Its sheltering shadow shall be shed.
Nations shall seek its pillar'd shade,
  Its leaves shall for their healing be ;
The circling flood that feeds its life,
  The blood that crimsoned Calvary.

42   TOPLADY. 7.

SAVIOUR of the human race !
  Magnify Thy power and grace ;
Let Thy kingdom come, we pray,
Let it come without delay ;
Cast down every rival throne,
And instead set up Thine own.

2 Since Thy kingdom is within,
And the rebel is our sin,
Let Thine arrows sharp and keen,

Pierce the enemy unseen;
Prince of Peace! the evil slay
That prevents Thy rightful sway.

3 Gird Thy sword upon Thy side,
O most Mighty One! and ride
O'er the prostrate hearts of foes,
Over all things that oppose;
Let Thy banner be unfurled
High above a conqered world.

ABRAHAM COLES.

43   HALLE. 7.

TAKE my life, and let it be
    Consecrated, Lord, to Thee.
Take my hands and let them move,
At the impulse of Thy love.
Take my feet and let them be
Swift and beautiful for Thee.

2 Take my voice and let me sing
Always, only, for my King,
Take my lips and let them be
Filled with messages from Thee.
Take my silver and my gold,
Not a mite would I withhold.

3 Take my moments and my days,
Let them flow in ceaseless praise.
Take my intellect, and use
Every power as Thou shalt choose.
Take my will and make it Thine;
It shall be no longer mine.

4 Take my heart it is Thine own;
It shall be Thy living throne.
Take my love; my Lord I pour
At Thy feet its treasure-store.
Take myself, and I will be
Ever, only, all for Thee.

FRANCES RIDLEY HAVERGAL.

44   LOVE AT HOME. 7, 5.

SET my anxious heart at rest,
  Lord, where dwellest Thou?
Deign to tell and end my quest,
  Lord, where dwellest Thou?
" If sincere Thy wish to know
Where My dwelling is below,
Listen, and I thee will show
  Where's My dwelling-place.

2 "Not in Holy Place and dim,
Is My dwelling-place :
Not between the Cherubim
Is My dwelling-place ;
O'er no Mercy Seat I shine,
Make no sacred chest My shrine ;
In no far off Palestine
Is My dwelling-place.

3 "In Eternity I dwell,
There's My dwelling-place :
In the contrite heart as well
There's My dwelling-place:
In the hearts of all that seek ;
With the merciful and meek,
Children, who My praises speak,
There's My dwelling-place.

ABRAHAM COLES.

45   EXPOSTULATION.   11.

BLEST land of Judea! thrice hallowed of song
    Where the holiest of memories pilgrim-like throng :
In the shade of thy palms, by the shores of thy sea,
On the hills of thy beauty, my heart is with thee.

2 With the eye of a spirit I look on that shore.
Where pilgrim and prophet have lingered before :
With the glide of a spirit I traverse the sod
Made bright by the steps of the angels of God.

3 Blue sea of the hills !—in my spirit I hear
Thy waters, Gennesaret, chime on my ear ;
Where the Lowly and Just with the people sat down
And thy spray on the dust of His sandals was thrown.

4 Lo, Bethlehem's hill-site before me is seen,
With the mountains around, and the valleys between ;
There rested the shepherds of Judah, and there
The song of the Angels rose sweet on the air.

5 And Bethany's palm trees in beauty still throw
Their shadows at noon on the ruins below :
But where are the sisters who hastened to greet
The lowly Redeemer, and sit at His feet ?

6 And throned on her hills sits Jerusalem yet,
But with dust on her forehead, and chains on her feet,
For the crown of her pride to the mocker hath gone,
And the holy Shechinah is dark where it shone.

7 I tread where the TWELVE in their wayfaring trod:
I stand where they stood with the CHOSEN OF GOD;
Where His blessing was heard and His lessons were
 taught,
Where the blind were restored and the healing was
 wrought.

8 And what if my feet may not tread where He stood,
Nor my ears hear the dashing of Galilee's flood,
Nor my eyes see the cross which He bowed Him to bear,
Nor my knees press Gethsemane's garden of prayer.

9 Yet loved of the Father, Thou, Jesus, art near
To the meek, and the lowly, and penitent, here:
And the voice of Thy love is the same even now.
As at Bethany's tomb, or on Olivet's brow.

JOHN G. WHITTIER.

46   LOUVAN.

THEY err who think that God is far,
 That I must climb from star to star,
Through mighty intervals of space,
To reach His awful dwelling-place.

2 I put the shoes from off my feet :
I go not forth my God to meet ;
For God is everywhere, and here,
Here in this place to make it dear.

3 Long time I groped and could not find ;
For light is darkness to the blind ;
How sweet to feel, now, He is found,
His everlasting arms around !

4 Upon His bosom thus to rest,
I cannot ask to be more blest ;
To know my sins are all forgiven
For Jesus' sake, O this is heaven !

5 While I love Him and He loves me,
I care no other heaven to see ;
And if there be some higher bliss,
I am content while I have this.

6 And there are those beyond the wave
Whom Christ came down on earth to save :
O let me haste to make it known,
My God and Saviour is their own.

ABRAHAM COLES

47   STABAT MATER. 8, 8, 7.

WICKED hands, how sad the story!
     Crucified the Lord of glory,
  Nailed Him to the accurse'd tree,
In Thy side the spear did bury,
Son of God, and Son of Mary !
  Murdered One of Calvary !

2 Was there ever known such malice?
Gall of hatred in the chalice
  For Thy lips of love wrung out ;
Priests with scribes and elders, mocking,
As they pass, O sight most shocking !
  Wag their heads, revile and flout.

3 Was there, Thine own words to borrow,
Ever sorrow like Thy sorrow,
  When our sins were on Thee laid !
Sorrow, which that cry could waken,
"Why, My God, am I forsaken ? "
  Never was since worlds were made.

4 Never after such dear fashion
Was there witnessed such compassion :
  Publish ye, who know the grace,
Make commanded proclamation
Of the Gospel of salvation
  To each creature of the race !

ABRAHAM COLES.

48   POLYCARP. 9, 6.

WHAT sound is this through heaven resound-
        ing ?
  God is Love, God is Love.

4 9

Jude 1. 25.

From earth I hear the sound rebounding,
   God is Love, God is Love.
Yes. while adoring hosts proclaim,
Love is His nature, Love His name,
My soul in rapture cries the same,
   God is Love, God is Love.

2 This song repeat, ye saints in glory,
   God is Love, God is Love.
And saints on earth shout back the story,
   God is Love, God is Love.
In this let heaven and earth agree
To sound His love both full and free,
And let the theme forever be,
   God is Love, God is Love.

3 Creation's thousand tongues proclaiming
   God is Love, God is Love.
And Providence unites exclaiming
   God is Love, God is Love.
But let the burdened sinner hear
The gospel sounding loud and clear,
To every soul both far and near,
   God is Love, God is Love.

49

HOLLEY. 7.

H ERE I labor, weak and lone,
Ever, ever sowing seed ;
Ever tending what is sown :
Little is my gain, indeed.

2 Oh, my Lord, the field is Thine :
Why do I, with empty pride,
Call the little garden mine,
When my work is Thine, beside ?

3 It I claim it for my own,
Thou wilt give me its poor gain ;
And, at harvest, I, alone,
May bring fruits to Thee in vain.

4 If I give myself to Thee
For Thy work, all poor and mean,
As Thou pleasest it shall be,
If I much or little glean.

5 Other work for me is none
But to do the Master's will ;
Wet with rain, or parched with sun,
Meekly I Thy garden till.

ROBERT LOWELL.

2 Peter 1. 11.

50   MIGDOL. L. M.

WHEN Jesus speaks, so sweet the sound,
     The harps of heaven are hushed to hear ;
And all His words go circling round
From lip to lip and ear to ear.

2 But wondering seraph never heard,
   In all the mighty years of heaven,
Music so sweet as that dear word ;
"Thy many sins are all forgiven."

3 Sinners of earth, redeemed by blood,
   How leaped your hearts, when first ye knew
Th' amazing grace, and understood
The gift of pardon was for you !

4 Adopted now, with spirits awed,
   Knowing your privilege unpriced,
Ye claim the fatherhood of God
And brotherhood of Jesus Christ.

                               ABRAHAM COLES.

51   UXBRIDGE. L. M.

LORD of all being ! throned afar,
    Thy glory flames from sun to star ;
Centre and soul of every sphere,
Yet to each loving heart how near !

2 Sun of our life, Thy quickening ray
Sheds on our path the glow of day ;
Star of our hope, Thy softened light
Cheers the long watches of the night.

3 Grant us Thy truth to make us free,
And kindling hearts that burn for Thee,
Till all Thy living altars claim
One holy light. one heavenly flame.

OLIVER WENDELL HOLMES.

52   KINNEY STREET.   9, 8.

FROM Thee, begetting sure conviction,
    Sound out, O risen Lord, always.
Those faithful words of valediction,
    " Lo! I am with you all the days :"
      REFRAIN.—All the days, all the days,
          " Lo! I am with you all the days."

2 What things shall happen on the morrow,
    Thou kindly hidest from our gaze ;
But tellest us in joy or sorrow,
    " Lo! I am with you all the days :"—REF.

3 When round our head the tempest rages,
    And sink our feet in miry ways,
Thy voice comes floating down the ages,
    " Lo! I am with you all the days :"—REF.

Hag. 2. 7.

4 O Thou who art our life and meetness,
   Not death shall daunt us nor amaze,
Hearing those words of power and sweetness,
   " Lo ! I am with you all the days :"—Ref.

ABRAHAM COLES.

53   SHINING SHORE.   8. 7.

YE messengers of God to men,
   Now on the deep sea tossing,
Naught shall you hurt, God shall avert
   The dangers of the crossing :
CHORUS.—Nothing to fear have ye, howe'er
         Loud ocean roars and ravens ;
      Let what winds blow, be glad to know,
         All ports are happy havens !

2 The ship is safe, with Christ ye sail,
   And ye are bearing orders ;
All places lie beneath one sky,
   Close to the heavenly borders :—CHO.

3 God at the helm to guide the bark,
   There is no room for error ;
Whom He has sent should be content,
   Nor yield to doubt nor terror :—CHO.

ABRAHAM COLES.

54   THE VALLEY OF BLESSING.   12, 7, 9, 8.

O'ER the ocean is wafted the tremulous cry,
   The cry of spirits in need :
" We are dying by millions, oh, let us not die !
   Come over and help us, we plead !
To famishing souls swiftest succor afford,
   The means of salvation us give ;
By the might of the Word of the Lord
   We then shall eternally live."

2 We hear blended with these far off pleadings
   of pain.
   The main's multitudinous moan ;
While th' importunate voice sighs again and again
   Its prayer in varying tone :
From many-hued people of different speech,
   The wail o'er the deep finds its way :
" We are dying, with life within reach,
   Come over and help us straightway !"

3 Who, unmoved, see their brother's deep lack,
   can there dwell
   The love of the Father in such ?
To whom much is forgiven, 'tis needful and well
   That they in return should love much.

Is. 63. 1.

Let frequent and fast-sailing ships never cease
  To plough, Lord, the furrowless sea,
To convey the Evangel of peace,
  Converting the world unto Thee.

ABRAHAM COLES.

55   St. PETERSBURGH. L. M.

GREAT Ruler of the land and sea,
  Almighty God we come to Thee;
Able to succor and to save
From perils of the wind and wave.
    CHORUS.—Keep by Thy mighty hand, Oh, keep,
        The dwellers on the homeless deep.

2 In storm or battle, with Thine arm
Shield Thou the mariner from harm ;
From foes without, from ills within,
From deeds and words and thoughts of sin.—CHO.

3 When hidden is each guiding star,
Flash out the beacon light afar ;
From mist and rock and shoal and spray.
Protect the sailor on his way.—CHO.

4 Defend from the quick lightning's stroke,
And from the iceberg's crushing shock ;
Take Thou the helm, and surely guide
The wanderer o'er the wayward tide.—CHO.

Is. 9 6.

5 Good Pilot of the awful main,
Let us not plead Thy love in vain ;
Jesus draw near with kindly aid,
Say. "It is I, be not afraid."—CHO.

HORATIUS BONAR.

56   CAN A LITTLE CHILD LIKE ME.   7.

CAN a little child, like me,
Thank the Father fittingly ?
Yes, oh yes ! be good and true.
Patient, kind in all you do ;
Love the Lord, and do your part,
Learn to say with all your heart :
    || Father, we thank Thee, ||
    Father in Heaven, we thank Thee !

2 For the fruit upon the tree,
For the birds that sing of Thee.
For the earth in beauty drest,
Father, mother, and the rest,
For Thy precious, loving care,
For Thy bounty everywhere,
    Father, we thank Thee ! etc.

MARY MAPES DODGE.

57   SWEET BY AND BY.   9.

HERE are partings and painful farewells,
And the sundering of tenderest ties ;

In that heavenly land where He dwells,
  God shall wipe away tears from all eyes.
Chorus.—In the sweet by and by,
    We shall meet on that beautiful shore.

2 Here the pilgrim can scarcely discern
  The reward for the tears that he sheds;
But the ransomed with songs shall return
  With everlasting joy on their heads.—Cho.

3 Guide the ship which Thy servants convey,
  Gracious Lord, o'er the turbulent foam:
Bless their labors, be with them alway,
  Till they reach the blest threshold of Home!

ABRAHAM COLES.

58   HARK! HARK, MY SOUL!   11, 10.

HARK! hark, my soul! angelic songs are swelling
  O'er earth's green fields and ocean's wave-beat
    shore:
How sweet the truth, those blessed strains are telling
  Of that new life when sin shall be no more!
Chorus—Angels of Jesus, angels of light,
      Singing to welcome the pilgrims of the night.

2 Onward we go, for still we hear them singing,
  "Come, weary souls, for Jesus bids you come;"
And thro' the dark, its echoes sweetly ringing,
  The music of the gospel leads us home.

3 Far, far away, like bells at evening pealing,
  The voice of Jesus sounds o'er land and sea :
And laden souls by thousands, meekly stealing,
  Kind Shepherd, turn their weary steps to Thee.

4 Rest comes at length, though life be long and dreary.
  The day must dawn, and darksome night be past :
All journeys end in welcome to the weary,
  And heaven, the heart's true home, will come at last.

Angels, sing on ! your faithful watches keeping,
  Sing us sweet fragments of the songs above,
Till morning's joy shall end the night of weeping,
  And life's long shadows break in cloudless love.

FREDERICK W. FABER.

59   HARK! THE SABBATH BELLS ARE RINGING.   8, 7.

EVERYWHERE the groves are ringing,
  In and out the warblers pass ;
Unseen insects join in singing
  Holy anthems from the grass.
CHORUS.—God who made us, downward gazes
      On His creatures, great and small,
    Condescends to hear the praises
      Of the meanest of them all.

2 Little is the bee that hovers,
  With its tiny wings and feet.
Lighting not till it discovers
  Where the blossom hides its sweet.—Cho.

3 As in mountain lake is given
  Image of the sky, we view
The same blessed arch of heaven
  Mirrored in a drop of dew.—Cho.

4 Therefore, O our God and Father,
  Little children though we be,
We around Thy throne would gather,
  Love and serve and worship Thee.—Cho.

5 We are sinful and unholy,
  Make the turbid waters clear,
That they may reflect Thee, solely,
  And display Thy likeness here.—Cho.

ABRAHAM COLES.

60   AUSTRIAN NATIONAL HYMN.   8, 7.

GOD of all, above and under,
  God of angels and of men;
All things praise Thee, Thine the Thunder,
  And the echoing Hills. Amen!

1 Tim. 2. 3.

Thine the worship of the Mountains :
　Thine the homage of the Plain ;
Thine the singing of the Fountains ;
　Thine the chorus of the Main.

2 Now while Heaven and Earth rejoices,
　God of heat, and God of cold!
With the tempest tune our voices,
　Hymning mercies new and old :
We would praise Thee, praise is comely,
　And an ever new delight ;
Lay our offerings, mean and homely,
　On Thine altar morn and night.

3 Sounding sweetly down the ages,
　Thy forgiving voice is heard,
Coming from the open pages
　Of the volume of Thy word :
For Thy love which changeth never.
　For Thy mercy to the race.
Blessed be Thy name forever.
　God of truth and God of grace!

ABRAHAM COLES.

61　　　　　MANOAH. C. M.

THOU God of Love! Thy glories bright
　The Universe adorn :

We see Thee in the stars of night,
    The splendors of the morn.

2 From east to west, from south to north,
    Thou dost in all appear;
But art supremely shadowed forth
    In Charity sincere.

3 Sweet Charity! divinest grace,
    Inclusive of the rest,
Pictures Thine image in the face
    And glorifies the breast.

4 Since it was this once caused to bleed
    Incarnate Deity,
To minister to suffering need
    Is to resemble Thee.

5 On great or small Thy hand bestows
    No higher honor, than
To make them channels through which flows
    Eternal life to man.

6 Thou wilt reward those seeking none;
    And make them wondering see
That what they to the least have done
    Was done alike to Thee.

ABRAHAM COLES.

John 6. 33.

62   Siloam.   C. M.

BLEST Lord, who hungry thousands fed,
   Look with a pitying eye,
Where fainting for the living bread,
   The heathen nations lie.

2 Light in our hearts that ardent flame
   Which brought Thee from above,
That we may long to teach Thy name,
   And glorify Thy love ;

3 That we may take the food divine,
   From Thy creating hands,
And, though unnumbered millions pine,
   Feed all the starving lands.

4 Grant that before Thy judgment seat
   No soul may have to say,
When Thou didst bid, " ' Give them to eat,'
   I hungry went away."
                      Mrs. Galusha Anderson.

63   Hebron.   L. M.

HAVE we not all one Father ?   Yea,—
   Hath not one God created us ?
How are we better then than they,
   Barbarians, not favored thus ?

6 3

2 He who bows down to stocks and stones,
   Brutish and ignorant and base,
With us a common nature owns,
   An upright form and heavenward face.

3 His coarser appetites may crave
   Coarse food on which his body feeds,
But he too has a soul to save,
   With similar immortal needs.

4 Despise not him for whom Christ died,
   However low despise him not:
Dear, doubtless, to the Crucified
   Is the benighted Hottentot.

ABRAHAM COLES.

64   SWEET HOUR OF PRAYER.   8.

HOW sweet the memory of those,
   Who toiled for Christ, and now repose
Beneath the soil their feet had trod,
While that they sowed the seed of God ;
In whom the Saviour's love so wrought,
They gave up all, and judged it nought ;
Deeming His smile made rich amends
For loss of country, home, and friends.

2 As instruments of Heaven's sweet will,
   Their delicate fingers used their skill

To couch the cataract of sin,
And let the welcome splendor in :
How glorious, when to eyes unsealed.
A heavenly beauty was revealed ;
By spiritual miracle of sight
Made conscious of a world of light!

3 What if no future sun should rise?
No morrow break in eastern skies?
For aye, to all of woman born
Were shut and sealed the gates of morn,
Streaked by no gleam of dawning light,
The endless horror of that night?
To weary watchers for the Day
What joy were in a single ray!

ABRAHAM COLES.

65   SPANISH HYMN. 7. DOUBLE.

ABBA, Father, God of love,
    Hallowed be Thy name, by all
In the height of heaven above,
    And on this terrestrial ball.
May Thy kingdom come in power,
    Subjugating all to Thee ;
Other kingdoms Thine devour
    That there only one may be.

2 May Thy righteous will be done
    By the fallen race of man,
Back to old allegiance won,
    Serving Thee as angels can.
Who have kept their first estate,
    And are strong and swift of wing,
Always eager and elate,
    Quick to bear and quick to bring.

3 Give our bodies needful food,
    Day by day their wants supply,
And withhold not heavenly food
    Lest our starving spirits die :
Man lives not by bread alone ;
    Should Thy blessing not attend
Bread's no better than a stone,
    Soon our mortal lives would end.

4 Debts to law and justice due,
    Freely cancel and forgive ;
Our revengeful souls renew
    That we may not die but live ;
Since, if we match not the grace
    Whereby Thou our sin dost blot,
Doubtful will be left the case
    Whether Thou forgiv'st or not.

5 For that we are weak and frail.
  Lead us not where danger lies ;
If the enemy assail,
  Let it not be a surprise.
In the dark and dreadful hour.
  From the Evil One deliver,
For the Kingdom's Thine and power,
  Now, hereafter, and forever.

ABRAHAM COLES.

66   TYROLESE AIR.   7.

L IFT to Him your hymns of laud,
   Who of gods alone is God !
CHORUS.—For His mercy, firm and sure,
      Doth from age to age endure.

2 Tune Him thanks with sounding chords,
Who doth reign the Lord of Lords :—CHO.

3 Who, by wisdom, made and bent
Overhead the firmament :—CHO.

4 Who the earth on nothing hung,
And in empty space it flung :—CHO.

5 Made the sun to rule the day,
And the joy of life convey :—CHO.

6 Moon and stars to rule the night
With a soft and mellow light:—Cho.

7 Who His chosen people led
Through the wilderness and fed :—Cho.

8 Who, when our estate was low,
Help remembered to bestow :—Cho.

9 Who to all flesh giveth food,
And abundance of all good :—Cho.

10 Let our thanks to Him be given,
Israel's God, the God of Heaven :—Cho.

ABRAHAM COLES.

67   ROCKINGHAM. L. M.

L ORD, visit Thy forsaken race,
      Back to Thy fold the wanderers bring ;
Teach them to seek Thy slighted grace.
      And hail in Christ their promised King.

2 The veil of darkness rend in twain,
      Which hides their Shiloh's glorious light,
The severed olive branch again
      Firm to its parent stock unite.

68   Centennial Anthem.   7.

L ET us to Jehovah raise
   Glad and grateful songs of praise !
Let the people with one voice
In the Lord their God rejoice :
    Chorus.—For His Mercy standeth fast,
           And from age to age doth last.

2 He across untraversed seas
Guided first the Genoese :
Here prepared a dwelling place
For a freedom-loving race :—Cho.

3 Filled the land, the red man trod,
With the worshippers of God :
When oppression forged the chain
Nerved their hands to rend in twain :—Cho.

4 Gave them courage to declare
What to do and what to dare :
Made them victors over wrong
In the battle with the strong :—Cho.

5 Midst the terror of the fight
Kept them steadfast in the right :
Taught their statesmen how to plan
To conserve the rights of man :—Cho.

6 Needful skill and wisdom lent
To establish government :
Laid foundations, resting still
On the granite of His will :—Cho.

7 Wiped the scandal and the sin
From the color of the skin :
Now o'er all, from sea to sea,
Floats the banner of the free :—Cho.

8 Down the ages rings the blow
Struck one hundred years ago :
Praise the Lord for freedom won,
And the Gospel of His Son :—Cho.

ABRAHAM COLES.

69   AMERICA. 6, 6, 4.

O BEAUTIFUL and grand,
My own, my native land !
Of thee I boast :
Great empire of the west,
The dearest and the best,
Made up of all the rest,
I love thee most.

2 Thou crown of all the past,
Times' noblest and the last,
Supremely fair :

Brought up at Freedom's knee,
Sweet child of Liberty,
Of all, from sea to sea,
　Th' undoubted heir.

3 I honor thee, because
Of just and equal laws,
　These make thee dear :
Not for thy mines of gold,
Not for thy wealth untold,
Not that thy sons are bold,
　Do I revere.

4 God of our fathers ! bless,
Exalt in righteousness
　This land of ours :
Be Right our lofty aim,
Our title and our claim
To high and higher fame
　Among the Powers.

ABRAHAM COLES.

70　　THE STAR SPANGLED BANNER.

WE hail each return of the day of thy birth,
　Fair Columbia, washed by the waves of two
　　oceans !
Where men from the farthest dominions of Earth

71

Rear altars to Freedom, and pay their devotions;
Where our fathers in fight, nobly strove for the Right,
Struck down their fierce foemen or put them to flight;
Through the long lapse of ages, that so there might be
An asylum for all in the Land of the Free.

2 Behold, from each zone under heaven they come!
    And haughtiest nations, that once far outshone thee,
Now paled by thy lustre, lie prostrate and dumb,
    And render due homage, and no more disown thee.
All the isles for thee wait, while that early and late,
Not a wind ever blows but wafts hither rich freight,
And the swift sailing ships, that bring over the sea
The oppressed of all lands to the Land of the Free.

3 As entranced I look down the long vista of years,
    And behold thine existence to ages extended,
What a scene. O my country, of wonder appears!
    How kindling the prospect, surpassing and splendid!
Each lone mountain and glen, and waste wilderness
        then,
I see covered with cities, and swarming with men,
And miraculous Art working marvels for thee
To lift higher thy greatness, thou Land of the Free!

4 From our borders expel all oppression and wrong,
  Oh Thou, who didst plant us and make us a nation !
In the strength of Thy arm make us evermore strong :
  On our gates inscribe Praise, on our walls write
    Salvation;
May Thyself be our light, from Thy heavenly height
Ever flashing new splendors and chasing our night,
That united and happy we ever may be
To the end of all time, still the Land of the Free !

ABRAHAM COLES.

71   "THANK GOD FOR THE BIBLE."

THANK God for the Bible ! 'tis there that we find
  The story of Christ and His love—
How He came down to earth from His beautiful home
  In the mansions of glory above.
      Thanks to Him we will bring,
      Praise to Him we will sing,
For He came down to earth from His beautiful home
  In the mansions of glory above.

2 While He lived on this earth to the sick and the blind
  And to mourners His blessings were given ;
And He said let the little ones come unto me,
  For of such is the kingdom of heaven.
      Jesus calls us to come,
      He's prepared us a home.

7 3

1 Cor. 1. 24.

For He said let the little ones come unto me
For of such is the kingdom of heaven.

3 In the Bible we read of a beautiful land,
  Where sorrow and pain never come;
For Jesus is there with a heavenly band
  And there has prepared us a home.
        Jesus calls, shall we stay?
        No! we'll gladly obey,
For Jesus is there with a heavenly band
  And there has prepared us a home.

4 Thank God for the Bible! its truths o'er the earth
  We'll scatter with bountiful hand;
But we never can tell what a Bible is worth
  Till we go to that beautiful land.
        There our thanks we will bring.
        There with angels we'll sing,
And its worth we can tell when with Jesus we dwell
  In heaven—that beautiful land.

72   BAXTER.   10.

HEAVEN is not reached at a single bound;
  But we build the ladder by which we rise,
  From the lowly earth to the vaulted skies,
And we mount to its summit round by round.

2 I count this thing to be grandly true:
That a noble deed is a step toward God,
Lifting the soul from the common clod
To a purer air and a broader view.

J. G. HOLLAND.

73   LENOX. 6. 8.

THE sweet prophetic Voice
    Tells every wind that blows,
The desert shall rejoice,
    And blossom as the rose;
The wilderness, no longer dumb,
Exultant sing, The Lord is come!

2 The uncultured wilds, where roams
    The Indian of the West,
Shall turn to happy homes
    And gardens of the blest;
The wilderness, no longer dumb,
Exultant sing, The Lord is come!

3 The pestilential swamp,
    Where slavery had root,
Shall, freed from noisome damp,
    Abound in wholesome fruit;
The wilderness no longer dumb,
Exultant sing, The Lord is come!

Is. 60. 20.

4 Hot Afric's barren sands,
  Where men stretch forth to God
Their supplicating hands,
  Shall change to verdant sod,
The wilderness, no longer dumb,
Exultant sing, The Lord is come!

5 Asia, the dwelling-place
  Of dragons, shall be clad
With plants and flowers of grace,
  And all her wastes be glad;
The wilderness, no longer dumb,
Exultant sing, The Lord is come!

6 And Europe's unfenced grounds,
  Where thorns and briars grow,
Shall leap through all her bounds—
  A Paradise below;
The wilderness, no longer dumb,
Exultant sing, The Lord is come!

7 Dear day of God, make haste!
  Let not the time be long
When sin no more shall waste,
  No more shall triumph wrong,
The wilderness, no longer dumb,
Exultant sing, The Lord is come!

ABRAHAM COLES.

74   Horton.   7s.

" GIVE us room that we may dwell,"
    Zion's children cry aloud ;
See their numbers how they swell,
    How they gather like a cloud !

2 Oh, how bright the morning seems,
    Brighter, from so darker night !
Zion is like one that dreams,
    Filled with wonder and delight.

3 Lo, thy sun goes down no more,
    God Himself will be thy light ;
All that caused thee grief before
    Buried lies in endless night.

4 Zion, now arise and shine,
    Lo, thy Light from heaven is come ;
These that crowd from far are thine,
    Give thy sons and daughters room !

75   Holy is the Lord.   9, 10.

HOLY, holy, holy is the Lord !
    Sing, O ye people, gladly adore Him ;
Let the mountains tremble at His word ;
    Let the hills be joyful before Him ;

Mighty in wisdom, boundless in mercy,
  Great is Jehovah, King over all.
CHORUS—Holy, holy, holy is the Lord,
    Let the hills be joyful before Him.

2 Praise Him, praise Him! shout aloud for joy,
  Watchman of Zion, herald the story ;
Sin and death His kingdom shall destroy,
  All the earth shall sing of His glory ;
Praise Him, ye angels, ye who behold Him,
  Robed in His splendor, matchless divine.—CHO.

3 King Eternal, blessed be His name!
  So may His children gladly adore Him,
When in heaven we join the happy strain,
  When we cast our bright crowns before Him ;
There in His likeness joyful awaking,
  There we shall see Him, there we shall sing,
CHORUS—Holy, holy, &c.

76   DENFIELD. C. M.

OUR Father, hear our longing prayer,
    And help this prayer to flow,
That humble thoughts which are Thy care,
  May live in us and grow.

Col. 1. 27.

2 For lowly hearts shall understand
    The peace, the calm delight
Of dwelling in Thy heavenly land,
    A pleasure in Thy sight.

3 Give us humility that so,
    Thy reign may come within,
And when Thy children homeward go,
    We too may enter in.

4 Hear us our Saviour! ours Thou art,
    Though we are not like Thee;
Give us Thy spirit in our heart,
    Large, lowly, trusting, free.

GEORGE MACDONALD.

GREENLAND. 8, 6.

OH! life is strange, and full of change,
    But it brings little sorrow;
For I came here but yesterday,
    And shall go hence to-morrow:

2 Go to the rest of the ever blest,
    To the New Jerusalem;
Children of light there walk in white,
    And the Saviour leadeth them.

JULIA WARD HOWE.

Rev. 5. 2.

78   BERLIN.   10.

N OW lift we Hymns of heart-felt praise to Thee,
   Our King, Redeemer, Saviour, Brother, Friend !
And when Thy face we, in Thy likeness, see,
Our adoration-song shall never end :

2 Then shall we sing—when with our God we reign,
Serving Thee, ever, in most holy ways—
" Worthy the Lamb who once for us was slain !"
That Song, forever new, of ceaseless praise.

3 While here we tarry in this world of need,
Seeking the lost ones who in darkness roam,
Thy little flock, Good Shepherd, gently lead,
And bear Thy lambs in safety to Thy Home.

E. S. C.

79   BETHANY.   6, 4.

E VER, my Lord, with Thee,
   Ever with Thee !
Through all eternity
   Thy face to see !
I count this heaven, to be
Ever, my Lord, with Thee,
   Ever with Thee !

Is. 33. 17.

2 Fair is Jerusalem,
   All of pure gold,
Garnished with many a gem
   Of worth untold :
I only ask, to be
Ever, my Lord, with Thee,
   Ever with Thee !

3 River of Life there flows
   As crystal clear ;
The Tree of Life there grows
   For healing near :
But this crowns all, to be
Ever, my Lord, with Thee,
   Ever with Thee !

4 No curse is there, no night,
   No grief. no fear ;
Thy smile fills heaven with light,
   Dries every tear :
What rapture, thère to be
Ever, my Lord, with Thee,
   Ever with Thee !

ABRAHAM COLES.

INDEX OF FIRST LINES OF HYMNS.

For convenience, a selection of Tunes has been made, (other tunes of course can be used, if desired). The majority of those given are such as can be found in the Standard Hymnals of the various denominations. The tunes " Polycarp" and " Tyrolese Air " are from " The Creation, a Service of Sacred Song," published by the London Sunday School Union. " Hark! hark, my Soul," set to music by W. F. Sherwin, " Love at Home" and " Rifted Rock " may be found in " Christian Songs for the Sunday School." " Holy, holy, holy is the Lord," in " Bright Jewels." " Over There," in " Songs for Little Folks." " The Valley of Blessing " and " The Sweet By and By," in " Gospel Hymns, No. 2." And the " Star Spangled Banner," " Shining Shore," " Sweet Hour of Prayer," " Love at Home," and " Hark! the Sabbath Bells," in Bradbury's " New Golden Chain."

Music to " Can a Little Child Like Me," may be found in St. Nicholas, Nov., 1877, permission to use the hymn having been kindly given by the publishers.

www.ingramcontent.com/pod-product-compliance
Lightning Source LLC
Chambersburg PA
CBHW020315090426
42735CB00009B/1347